Building a Sustainable Future

The Growing Impact of ESG Integration in Investment Decisions

Richard R. Alexander

Table of Contents

Introduction to Green Finance and Sustainable Investments

In recent years, the global community has witnessed an increasing awareness of environmental issues and the urgent need to address climate change, resource depletion, and other ecological challenges. As a result, there has been a growing emphasis on incorporating sustainability and responsible practices into various sectors of society, including finance and investments. Green finance and sustainable investments have emerged as critical concepts that aim to align financial decisions with environmentally and socially responsible goals.

Understanding the Need for Responsible Financial Practices:

Traditional financial practices have often prioritized short-term gains and profits without considering the long-term consequences on the environment and society. This approach has led to the exploitation of natural resources, the degradation of ecosystems, and social inequalities. The need for responsible financial practices arises from the realization that these unsustainable actions are not only detrimental to the planet but also pose risks to the stability of the global economy.

Defining Green Finance:

Green finance refers to the integration of environmental and social considerations into financial decision-making processes. It involves directing capital and investments towards projects, businesses, and initiatives that promote sustainable development, support clean technologies, and minimize negative impacts on the environment. Green finance encompasses a wide range of financial instruments, policies, and initiatives designed to address environmental challenges while providing financial returns to investors.

Exploring Sustainable Investments:

Sustainable investments are a subset of green finance and involve allocating funds to businesses, organizations, or projects that adhere to environmentally and socially responsible practices. These investments not only seek to generate financial returns for investors but also strive to create positive impacts on the planet and communities. Sustainable investments can take various forms, including green bonds, social impact bonds, sustainable mutual funds, and venture capital in green startups.

Key Principles of Green Finance and Sustainable Investments:

- **Environmental, Social, and Governance (ESG) Factors:** ESG criteria are used to evaluate the sustainability and ethical impact of investments. Environmental factors consider a company's carbon footprint, water usage, and waste management. Social factors assess labor practices, community relations, and diversity and inclusion. Governance factors examine the company's leadership, transparency, and accountability.

- **Risk Management:** Green finance acknowledges the risks associated with climate change, resource scarcity, and shifting regulatory landscapes. By factoring these risks into investment decisions, investors can better safeguard their portfolios from potential shocks and uncertainties.

- **Impact Measurement and Reporting:** Sustainable investments focus on measurable positive impacts on environmental and social issues. Investors seek transparency and accountability through impact reporting to ensure that their investments align with their desired outcomes.

- **Innovation and Technology:** Green finance promotes the adoption of innovative technologies and solutions that support sustainability goals. This includes investments in renewable energy, energy-efficient infrastructure, and eco-friendly innovations.

Benefits of Green Finance and Sustainable Investments:

1. **Environmental Benefits:** By channeling funds into eco-friendly projects, green finance contributes to the conservation of natural resources, reduction of greenhouse gas emissions, and the protection of biodiversity.

2. **Social Benefits:** Sustainable investments support businesses that prioritize fair labor practices, community development, and social well-being, leading to more inclusive and equitable societies.

3. **Financial Returns:** Contrary to the misconception that sustainable investments yield lower returns, numerous studies suggest that companies with strong ESG performance often outperform their

counterparts over the long term, indicating that responsible financial practices can be financially rewarding.

4. **Risk Mitigation:** By identifying and addressing environmental and social risks, green finance helps reduce the vulnerability of investments to external shocks, such as regulatory changes or reputational damage.

In conclusion, green finance and sustainable investments are essential components of transitioning towards a more sustainable and responsible financial system. By integrating environmental, social, and governance factors into investment decisions, we can create a positive impact on the world while achieving financial prosperity in a changing global landscape. As the awareness of climate change and social responsibility continues to grow, these concepts are likely to play an increasingly significant role in shaping the future of finance and investment practices.

The Rise of Sustainable Finance:

A Paradigm Shift in Investment Strategies

Sustainable finance represents a transformative shift in the world of investment strategies, where environmental, social, and governance (ESG) considerations are integrated into financial decision-making processes. This shift is driven by the recognition that traditional investment approaches often neglected the long-term impacts of businesses and projects on the environment and society. The rise of sustainable finance marks a departure from purely profit-driven motives to a more holistic and responsible approach that aims to generate positive outcomes for both investors and the planet.

Evolution of Sustainable Finance:

Historically, financial markets primarily focused on short-term financial gains, with little emphasis on the consequences of investments on the environment and communities. However, as environmental issues like climate change, resource depletion, and pollution intensified, and social concerns such as income inequality and labor practices gained attention, investors began to recognize the significance of ESG factors in their decision-making. Over time, a paradigm shift occurred, and sustainable finance emerged as a response to the growing need for more responsible investment practices. This shift is seen as a win-win situation, where investors can achieve their financial objectives while contributing to positive environmental and social outcomes.

Incorporating ESG Factors:

At the core of sustainable finance lies the integration of ESG factors into investment strategies. Let's explore each component:

- **Environmental Factors:** These encompass a wide range of considerations, including a company's carbon footprint, energy efficiency, waste management, water usage, and commitment to biodiversity conservation. Investments in renewable energy, green technologies, and sustainable agriculture are examples of environmentally conscious choices.

- **Social Factors:** Social considerations examine a company's impact on employees, customers, suppliers, and the broader community. Evaluating labor practices, human rights, diversity and inclusion, and community engagement helps identify socially responsible investments.

- **Governance Factors:** Governance refers to a company's leadership, transparency, accountability, and adherence to ethical business practices. Investors seek companies with robust corporate governance structures and practices to mitigate risks and ensure responsible decision-making.

Sustainable Investment Vehicles:

The rise of sustainable finance has led to the development of various investment vehicles tailored to align with ESG principles:

- **Green Bonds:** Green bonds are debt instruments issued by companies or governments to finance environmentally friendly projects. The funds raised are dedicated to initiatives such as renewable energy projects, clean transportation, or sustainable infrastructure.

- **Social Impact Bonds:** Social impact bonds, also known as pay-for-success bonds, provide funding for projects that address social issues. Investors receive returns based on the successful achievement of predefined social outcomes.

- **Sustainable Mutual Funds:** These are investment funds that pool money from multiple investors to invest in a diversified portfolio of sustainable companies and projects. Sustainable mutual funds consider ESG factors when selecting investments.

- **ESG Index Funds:** ESG index funds track stock market indices composed of companies that meet specific sustainability criteria. These funds aim to replicate the performance of the underlying index while adhering to ESG principles.

Institutional Adoption and Regulation:

The rise of sustainable finance has gained significant momentum due to increased institutional adoption. Institutional investors, such as pension funds, sovereign wealth funds, and asset management firms, have integrated ESG considerations into their investment strategies to align with the values of their stakeholders and to manage long-term risks effectively.
Furthermore, regulators and policymakers have recognized the importance of sustainable finance in addressing global challenges. They have started implementing measures to encourage sustainable practices, such as mandating ESG reporting, setting disclosure requirements, and

offering tax incentives for green investments.

The Business Case for Sustainable Finance:

Contrary to the perception that sustainable investments may underperform, evidence suggests that companies with strong ESG performance often exhibit better long-term financial performance and risk management. Companies focused on sustainable practices are better equipped to adapt to changing market conditions, regulatory shifts, and societal expectations, making them more resilient and attractive to investors.

Moreover, the demand for sustainable products and services from environmentally and socially conscious consumers continues to grow, creating new market opportunities for sustainable businesses and driving investor interest.

Conclusion:

The rise of sustainable finance marks a paradigm shift in investment strategies, where ESG considerations have become integral to decision-making processes. Investors and financial institutions are increasingly recognizing that addressing environmental and social challenges can lead to better financial outcomes while fostering a more sustainable and equitable world. As sustainable finance continues to gain prominence, it has the potential to reshape the global financial landscape and contribute significantly to addressing pressing global challenges.

Green Bonds:

Accelerating the Transition to a Low-Carbon Economy

Green bonds have emerged as a powerful financial instrument aimed at funding projects and initiatives that promote environmental sustainability and contribute to the transition to a low-carbon economy. These bonds offer a unique opportunity for governments, corporations, and institutions to raise capital for projects that have positive environmental impacts. By attracting investors seeking to align their portfolios with environmentally responsible ventures, green bonds play a crucial role in accelerating the global transition towards a more sustainable future.

Definition and Characteristics of Green Bonds:

Green bonds are debt securities issued by governments, municipalities, corporations, or financial institutions to raise capital specifically for projects and activities with environmental benefits. Unlike traditional bonds, the proceeds from green bonds are earmarked exclusively for green projects. These projects typically focus on renewable energy, energy efficiency, sustainable transportation, climate adaptation, biodiversity conservation, and other environmentally friendly initiatives.

Characteristics of Green Bonds include:

1. Use of Proceeds: The issuer of a green bond must specify the intended use of the funds, which must be dedicated exclusively to green projects or assets.

2. External Review and Certification:
Many green bonds undergo external reviews by third-party verifiers to ensure compliance with defined green criteria and standards. This certification adds credibility and transparency to the bond's green nature.

3. Reporting and Transparency:
Issuers often commit to providing regular updates and reports on the progress and impact of the projects funded by the green bonds, ensuring transparency for investors and stakeholders.

4. Green Bond Framework: Some
issuers establish a Green Bond Framework, outlining their environmental objectives and criteria for selecting eligible projects.

Benefits of Green Bonds:

1. Financing Sustainable Projects:
Green bonds provide a direct channel for

financing projects that promote sustainability and contribute to climate change mitigation and adaptation. This funding is vital in supporting the development and implementation of green initiatives.

2. Mobilizing Capital: By tapping into the global capital market, green bonds have the potential to mobilize significant amounts of capital from a diverse range of investors, including institutional investors, asset managers, and environmentally conscious individuals.

3. Diversification of Investors: Green bonds attract investors seeking to incorporate ESG principles into their portfolios, expanding the investor base and diversifying the sources of funding for green projects.

4. Enhanced Reputation and Branding: Issuers of green bonds often benefit from enhanced reputation and branding as they demonstrate a commitment to sustainability and responsible corporate practices.

5. Risk Mitigation: By investing in projects that address environmental challenges, green bonds help mitigate long-term risks associated with climate change, resource depletion, and regulatory shifts.

Key Players in the Green Bond Market:

1. Governments and Municipalities: Many countries and municipalities issue green bonds to fund renewable energy projects, sustainable transportation infrastructure, and climate adaptation measures.

2. Corporations: Companies across various industries, such as renewable energy, clean technology, and sustainable agriculture, issue green bonds to finance their environmentally friendly projects.

3. Multilateral Development Banks (MDBs): MDBs like the World Bank and the European Investment Bank issue green bonds to fund projects that promote sustainable development in various regions.

4. Financial Institutions: Banks and other financial institutions also participate in the green bond market as both issuers and investors, aligning their investments with ESG principles.

Growth of the Green Bond Market:

The green bond market has experienced significant growth over the years. According to data from the Climate Bonds Initiative, the issuance of green bonds surpassed $500 billion in 2020. As governments and companies increasingly commit to sustainability goals and investors prioritize ESG considerations, the green bond market is expected to continue expanding.

Challenges and Future Outlook:

- **Standardization:** The lack of standardized definitions and frameworks for green projects could lead to ambiguity and "greenwashing," where issuers exaggerate the environmental benefits of their projects. Establishing clear and consistent green bond standards is crucial for maintaining investor confidence.

- **Market Liquidity:** While the green bond market has grown, it is still relatively smaller compared to the overall bond market. Increasing market liquidity and diversifying the range of green bond issuers will attract more investors and further accelerate the transition to a low-carbon economy.

- **Regulatory Support:** Encouraging regulatory frameworks, tax incentives, and policy support from governments can foster the growth of the green bond market and incentivize issuers to invest in sustainable projects.

Conclusion:

Green bonds have emerged as a vital financial instrument in the fight against climate change and the transition to a low-carbon economy. By channeling funds into projects that promote environmental sustainability, green bonds mobilize capital from diverse investors and facilitate the implementation of critical initiatives. As the world intensifies its efforts to combat climate change and address environmental challenges, the green bond market is poised to play an increasingly significant role in driving the transition towards a more sustainable and resilient future.

ESG Integration in Investment Decisions:

A Roadmap for Responsible Investing

ESG integration in investment decisions refers to the incorporation of Environmental, Social, and Governance factors into the process of evaluating and selecting investments. This approach goes beyond traditional financial metrics to consider a broader set of criteria that assess the environmental and social impacts of a company or project, as well as its governance practices. ESG integration aims to promote responsible investing, create positive social and environmental outcomes, and manage long-term risks more effectively.

Understanding ESG Factors:

- **Environmental Factors:**
  Environmental considerations involve

assessing a company's impact on the environment. This includes its carbon footprint, energy efficiency, waste management practices, water usage, and efforts towards mitigating climate change. Investments in renewable energy, clean technologies, and sustainable resource management are examples of environmentally responsible choices.

- **Social Factors:** Social considerations focus on a company's relationships with its employees, customers, suppliers, and the communities in which it operates. Key areas of assessment include labor practices, employee relations, diversity and inclusion, product safety, customer satisfaction, and community engagement. Socially responsible investments prioritize companies that prioritize fair treatment, social well-being, and community development.

- **Governance Factors:** Governance factors pertain to a company's leadership, board structure, transparency, and adherence to ethical business practices. Strong corporate governance is vital for maintaining investor trust and ensuring that companies make responsible decisions. ESG integration looks for companies with robust governance frameworks and independent boards.

The Case for ESG Integration in Investment Decisions:

- **Risk Management:** Integrating ESG factors in investment decisions helps identify and manage risks that might not be apparent from traditional financial analysis. For example, companies with weak environmental practices may face regulatory fines or reputational damage, while those with poor labor practices may encounter employee strikes or legal disputes. ESG integration enables investors to mitigate these risks effectively.

- **Long-Term Performance:** Companies that prioritize ESG considerations tend to exhibit better long-term financial performance. By addressing environmental and social issues proactively, these companies are better equipped to navigate changing market dynamics and evolving consumer preferences.

- **Stakeholder Trust:** Responsible investing fosters trust among stakeholders, including investors, customers, employees, and the general public. Demonstrating a commitment to sustainability and ethical practices enhances a company's reputation and can lead to increased loyalty and support.

- **Alignment with Global Goals:** ESG integration aligns investments with broader global goals, such as the United Nations Sustainable Development Goals (SDGs) and the Paris Agreement on climate change. Investing in projects and companies that contribute positively to these goals has a significant impact on addressing pressing global challenges.

Implementing ESG Integration:

a. Data Collection and Analysis: ESG integration requires access to relevant data on companies' environmental, social, and governance performance. This data can be sourced from company reports, third-party ESG research providers, and industry databases. Rigorous analysis of this information is essential to assess the ESG performance of potential investments accurately.

b. Engagement and Active Ownership: Engaging with companies in which investments are made is a crucial aspect of ESG integration. Active ownership involves constructive dialogue with company management to influence positive change, promote sustainable practices, and address ESG-related issues.

c. ESG Metrics and Scoring: Investors often use ESG metrics and scoring systems to compare and rank companies based on their ESG performance. These tools facilitate the evaluation and comparison of potential investments based on their sustainability and responsible business practices.

d. ESG Integration in Portfolio Construction: ESG considerations can be integrated into portfolio construction through various strategies, such as positive screening (selecting companies with strong ESG performance), negative screening (excluding companies involved in controversial industries), and thematic investing (focusing on specific ESG themes, such as renewable energy).

Challenges and Future Outlook:

a. Data Quality and Availability: Ensuring the accuracy and consistency of ESG data can be challenging, as it often relies on voluntary disclosures by companies. The standardization and improvement of ESG reporting are essential for effective ESG integration.

b. Lack of Industry Standards: The absence of universal ESG standards and definitions can lead to discrepancies in how ESG criteria are interpreted and applied. The development of common standards and frameworks is essential for promoting consistent ESG integration practices.

c. Regulation and Policy: The role of regulators and policymakers is critical in promoting ESG integration. Supportive regulations and policies can incentivize companies to disclose ESG information and encourage investors to prioritize responsible investing.

Conclusion:

ESG integration in investment decisions represents a roadmap for responsible investing that goes beyond financial metrics to consider environmental, social, and governance factors. By aligning investments with sustainability and ethical principles, ESG integration offers the potential for improved risk management, long-term financial performance, and positive social and environmental outcomes. As the importance of sustainability and responsible practices continues to grow, ESG integration is likely to become an increasingly central aspect of investment strategies worldwide.

Impact-Driven Initiatives:

Fostering Positive Social and Environmental Change through Finance

Impact-driven initiatives represent a growing movement within the financial sector that seeks to generate positive social and environmental outcomes alongside financial returns. These initiatives aim to leverage finance as a powerful tool to address pressing global challenges, such as poverty, inequality, climate change, and environmental degradation. By directing capital towards projects and businesses with explicit social and environmental objectives, impact-driven initiatives foster positive change and contribute to a more sustainable and equitable world.

Types of Impact-Driven Initiatives:

- **Impact Investing:** Impact investing involves deploying capital into companies, organizations, or funds that have a clear social or environmental mission. Investors actively seek measurable positive impacts alongside financial returns. This approach goes beyond traditional philanthropy, as it aims to achieve both financial and social/environmental goals simultaneously.

- **Socially Responsible Investing (SRI):** Socially responsible investing entails aligning investment decisions with individual values and ethical considerations. SRI investors may avoid investing in industries deemed harmful, such as tobacco, weapons, or fossil fuels, and instead focus on companies with strong ESG practices.

- **Community Development Finance:** Community development finance aims to provide financial resources to underserved communities and projects that enhance economic and social well-being. This form of finance often targets projects related to affordable housing, small businesses, education, and healthcare in marginalized areas.

- **Green Finance:** Green finance specifically focuses on funding environmentally sustainable projects and initiatives. This includes investments in renewable energy, energy efficiency, sustainable agriculture, waste management, and conservation efforts.

Measuring Impact:

Effectively measuring the impact of these initiatives is a critical aspect of impact-driven finance. Various methodologies and frameworks are used to assess and quantify the social and environmental effects of investments. Some common approaches include:

1. Social Return on Investment (SROI): SROI is a methodology that quantifies the social value created by an investment. It involves measuring the social outcomes and assigning a financial value to these impacts, allowing for a comparison of the social return to the financial investment.

2. Impact Reporting and Investment Standards (IRIS): IRIS is a set of metrics developed by the Global Impact Investing Network (GIIN) that provides standardized indicators for measuring and reporting the social and environmental performance of impact investments.

3. United Nations Sustainable Development Goals (SDGs): The SDGs serve as a global framework for addressing the world's most significant challenges by 2030. Impact-driven initiatives often align with specific SDGs to guide their objectives and measure their contributions to sustainable development.

Role of Financial Institutions and Investors:

Financial institutions, including banks, asset managers, and private equity firms, play a crucial role in driving impact-driven initiatives. They act as intermediaries between investors and impact projects, facilitating the flow of capital towards impactful opportunities. Some ways financial institutions contribute to impact-driven finance include:

- **Developing Impact Funds:**
  Financial institutions create and
  manage impact investment funds that
  pool capital from multiple investors to
  support a diverse range of impactful
  projects.

- **Impact Screening:** They implement
  impact screening processes to assess
  and identify investments that align
  with their impact objectives.

- **Impact Measurement and
  Reporting:** Financial institutions
  establish systems for measuring and
  reporting the social and
  environmental outcomes of their
  impact investments to stakeholders,
  ensuring transparency and
  accountability.

- **Engaging in Impact Advocacy:**
  Some financial institutions engage in

advocacy efforts to promote policies and regulations that support impact-driven initiatives.

Challenges and Opportunities:

- **Data and Measurement:** The lack of standardized impact measurement and reporting practices presents challenges for investors and stakeholders seeking to evaluate the true impact of investments.

- **Scalability:** Scaling up impact-driven initiatives can be challenging, particularly in addressing large-scale global issues like climate change and poverty.

- **Risk and Return Trade-Off:** Balancing financial returns with impact objectives can be complex. Impact-driven initiatives aim to demonstrate that positive social and environmental outcomes can be achieved without sacrificing financial performance.

- **Policy and Regulatory Support:** Supportive policies and regulatory frameworks are essential to create an enabling environment for impact-driven initiatives to thrive.

Conclusion:

Impact-driven initiatives are reshaping the finance landscape, emphasizing the importance of investing in projects and businesses that create positive social and environmental change. By aligning financial objectives with social and environmental goals, impact-driven finance represents a promising path towards a more sustainable and equitable future. As the momentum for impact-driven finance continues to grow, its potential to drive positive change on a global scale becomes increasingly significant.

Sustainable Investing:

Aligning Profitability with Environmental and Social Goals

Sustainable investing, also known as socially responsible investing (SRI) or responsible investing, is an investment approach that seeks to align financial goals with environmental, social, and governance (ESG) considerations. It goes beyond traditional financial metrics to evaluate the impact of investments on the planet and society. Sustainable investing aims to generate positive outcomes for both investors and the world by supporting companies and projects that prioritize sustainability, ethical practices, and responsible governance.

The Evolution of Sustainable Investing:

Sustainable investing has evolved over time, driven by the growing awareness of environmental and social challenges. Initially, ethical considerations were the primary focus, where investors excluded certain industries, such as tobacco or weapons, from their portfolios based on ethical beliefs. However, the scope of sustainable investing has broadened to encompass ESG factors that assess the overall sustainability and impact of investments.

Key Components of Sustainable Investing:

- **Environmental Factors:** This component evaluates a company's impact on the environment, including its carbon emissions, energy efficiency, waste management, water usage, and adherence to sustainable practices. Investments in renewable energy, clean technologies, and sustainable agriculture are examples of environmentally conscious choices.

- **Social Factors:** Social considerations assess a company's relationships with its employees, customers, suppliers, and communities. Areas of evaluation include labor practices, employee well-being, product safety, customer satisfaction, and community engagement. Sustainable investing favors companies that prioritize fair treatment, diversity and inclusion, and positive social impacts.

- **Governance Factors:** Governance involves examining a company's leadership, board structure, transparency, and adherence to ethical business practices. Strong corporate governance is critical for building trust with stakeholders and ensuring responsible decision-making.

Sustainable Investment Strategies:

- **Positive Screening:** Positive screening involves actively selecting companies or projects with strong ESG performance and sustainability practices. Investors proactively seek opportunities that align with their environmental and social values.

- **Negative Screening:** Negative screening excludes companies engaged in activities considered harmful to the environment or society. Common exclusions may include fossil fuel extraction, tobacco, weapons, or companies involved in human rights violations.

- **Thematic Investing:** Thematic investing focuses on specific ESG themes or sustainability issues. Examples include investing in clean energy, water scarcity solutions, or gender equality initiatives.

- **Impact Investing:** Impact investing targets investments that have a measurable and intentional positive impact on specific social or environmental outcomes. The aim is to generate both financial returns and positive social change.

Benefits of Sustainable Investing:

1. Mitigating Long-Term Risks: By considering ESG factors, sustainable investing helps investors identify and manage risks related to climate change, resource scarcity, regulatory changes, and reputational damage.

2. Long-Term Financial Performance:
Contrary to the belief that sustainable investing sacrifices returns, studies have shown that companies with strong ESG performance often exhibit better long-term financial performance.

3. Positive Environmental and Social Outcomes: Sustainable investing channels funds into companies and projects that promote sustainability and contribute to positive social and environmental outcomes.

5. Stakeholder Engagement:
Sustainable investing fosters meaningful engagement between investors and companies, encouraging companies to adopt more responsible practices and transparency.

Challenges and Future Outlook:

- **Data and Measurement:** The lack of standardized and consistent ESG data remains a challenge for sustainable investing. Efforts to improve data quality and reporting are ongoing.

- **Greenwashing:** Greenwashing refers to companies overstating or misrepresenting their environmental or social efforts to appear more sustainable than they are. Investors must exercise due diligence to avoid falling victim to greenwashing.

- **Policy and Regulatory Support:** Supportive policies and regulations are essential to promote sustainable investing and encourage greater transparency and disclosure.

Conclusion:

Sustainable investing represents a powerful approach to aligning profitability with environmental and social goals. By integrating ESG considerations into investment decisions, investors can contribute to positive change while achieving financial returns. As sustainable investing gains momentum, it has the potential to drive corporate responsibility, foster innovation in sustainable practices, and play a significant role in addressing global challenges such as climate change and social inequality.

ESG Metrics and Reporting:

Measuring the Impact of Sustainable Investments

ESG metrics and reporting play a crucial role in sustainable investing by providing a standardized and comprehensive framework to assess the environmental, social, and governance (ESG) performance of companies and investments. These metrics enable investors to evaluate the sustainability and responsibility of their portfolios and measure the impact of sustainable investments on the environment and society. ESG reporting enhances transparency, accountability, and decision-making, empowering investors to make informed choices that align financial goals with positive environmental and social outcomes.

Importance of ESG Metrics and Reporting:

1. Measurement and Comparison: ESG metrics allow investors to quantify the impact of their investments on various sustainability factors. It enables them to compare the performance of different companies or projects based on their ESG performance, facilitating better investment decisions.

2. Risk Management: ESG metrics help identify potential risks related to environmental and social factors that may impact the long-term viability of investments. By addressing these risks, investors can enhance the resilience of their portfolios.

3. Impact Assessment: ESG reporting measures the positive environmental and social outcomes of sustainable investments. It helps investors understand the real-world contributions of their investments to sustainability goals.

Types of ESG Metrics:

- **Environmental Metrics:** These metrics assess a company's environmental impact, such as carbon emissions, energy usage, water consumption, waste management, and biodiversity conservation efforts. Key environmental metrics include carbon intensity (carbon emissions per revenue or unit of production), water usage efficiency, and renewable energy usage.

- **Social Metrics:** Social metrics evaluate a company's performance in areas such as labor practices, employee well-being, product safety, community engagement, and diversity and inclusion. Social metrics may include employee turnover rates,

gender and racial diversity within the
workforce, community development
investments, and philanthropic
contributions.

- **Governance Metrics:** Governance
  metrics focus on the company's
  management, leadership, and ethical
  practices. These metrics assess board
  independence, executive
  compensation alignment,
  anti-corruption measures, and the
  strength of corporate governance
  structures.

**ESG Reporting Standards and
Frameworks:**

a. Global Reporting Initiative (GRI):
GRI provides a widely recognized reporting
framework that helps companies and
organizations disclose their ESG
performance. The GRI standards offer
comprehensive guidelines for reporting on

economic, environmental, and social impacts.

b. Sustainability Accounting Standards Board (SASB): SASB provides industry-specific ESG reporting standards to help companies disclose financially material sustainability information to investors.

c. Task Force on Climate-related Financial Disclosures (TCFD): TCFD offers recommendations for climate-related financial disclosures to help companies assess and disclose climate-related risks and opportunities.

d. United Nations Sustainable Development Goals (SDGs): The SDGs serve as a global framework for sustainable development. Companies and investors often align their ESG reporting with specific SDGs to measure their contributions to global sustainability goals.

Challenges in ESG Metrics and Reporting:

a. Data Availability and Quality: Collecting reliable and consistent ESG data remains a challenge, as it often relies on voluntary disclosures by companies. Improving data quality and availability is crucial for accurate reporting.

b. Standardization: The lack of standardized ESG metrics and reporting formats can lead to discrepancies in how companies report their sustainability performance. Standardizing reporting practices across industries and regions can enhance comparability.

c. Greenwashing: Some companies may engage in greenwashing, where they overstate their ESG efforts to appear more sustainable than they actually are. Robust reporting frameworks and third-party verification can help address greenwashing concerns.

Advancing ESG Metrics and Reporting:

a. Regulatory Support: Supportive policies and regulations that mandate ESG reporting can encourage greater transparency and accountability in sustainable investing.

b. Investor Engagement: Investors can actively engage with companies to encourage ESG disclosures and improve the quality of reported data.

c. Collaboration and Industry Initiatives: Collaborative efforts among companies, investors, and standard-setting organizations can drive the adoption of common ESG metrics and reporting standards.

Conclusion:

ESG metrics and reporting are essential tools in sustainable investing, enabling investors to measure and assess the environmental, social, and governance performance of their investments. By providing transparency and quantifiable data, ESG reporting empowers investors to make informed decisions that align financial objectives with positive environmental and social impacts. As the focus on sustainability and responsible investing grows, the advancement of ESG metrics and reporting will continue to play a pivotal role in fostering a more sustainable and equitable future.

The Role of Institutional Investors in Advancing Green Finance

Institutional investors, such as pension funds, insurance companies, sovereign wealth funds, and asset management firms, manage significant pools of capital on behalf of their clients and beneficiaries. Given their vast financial resources and long-term investment horizons, institutional investors play a crucial role in advancing green finance. Green finance aims to direct capital towards environmentally sustainable projects and initiatives that address climate change, promote renewable energy, and support the transition to a low-carbon economy. The engagement and commitment of institutional investors are vital in driving the global transition towards a more sustainable and resilient future.

Capital Allocation to Green Investments:

One of the primary roles of institutional investors in advancing green finance is allocating capital to green investments. By actively investing in green bonds, renewable energy projects, sustainable infrastructure, and other environmentally friendly assets, institutional investors contribute to financing initiatives that promote sustainability and address climate-related challenges. This capital allocation not only provides financial support but also signals to the market the demand for sustainable investments.

ESG Integration in Investment Strategies:

Institutional investors can integrate environmental, social, and governance (ESG) factors into their investment strategies. By considering ESG criteria in their decision-making processes, investors can identify and select companies and projects that prioritize sustainability and responsible practices. ESG integration helps manage risks associated with environmental and social issues while seeking to generate long-term value for investors.

Active Ownership and Engagement:

Institutional investors, as major shareholders of companies, have the power to influence corporate behavior and practices through active ownership and engagement. They can engage with companies in their portfolios to encourage improvements in ESG performance, corporate governance, and sustainability reporting. By exercising their voting rights and participating in shareholder resolutions, institutional investors can advocate for positive changes and hold companies accountable for their environmental impacts.

Support for Green Bonds and Impact Investing:

Institutional investors can act as significant buyers and issuers of green bonds, which are debt securities specifically designed to finance environmentally sustainable projects. By investing in green bonds, institutional investors contribute directly to funding projects that promote renewable energy, energy efficiency, and other green initiatives. Additionally, they can create and manage impact investing funds that target investments with measurable positive social and environmental outcomes.

ESG Reporting and Transparency:

Institutional investors play a critical role in promoting ESG reporting and transparency among the companies they invest in. They can request companies to disclose comprehensive ESG information, set clear reporting expectations, and use standardized reporting frameworks. This information allows investors to assess the ESG performance of their portfolios and make informed decisions based on sustainability criteria.

Advocacy and Policy Support:

Institutional investors have the potential to influence policy and regulatory frameworks that support green finance. By collaborating with governments, industry associations, and other stakeholders, they can advocate for policies that incentivize sustainable investments, provide tax benefits for green projects, and encourage corporate sustainability practices. Policy advocacy can create an enabling environment for green finance to flourish.

Collaboration and Knowledge Sharing:

Institutional investors can leverage their collective influence by collaborating with other investors, organizations, and initiatives focused on green finance. Sharing best practices, experiences, and knowledge enables the development of innovative and effective approaches to advance sustainability goals. Collaborative efforts can also lead to the creation of new investment products and strategies that drive positive environmental and social impact.

Conclusion:

Institutional investors play a pivotal role in advancing green finance and contributing to a more sustainable and resilient global economy. By directing capital towards environmentally sustainable projects, integrating ESG criteria into investment decisions, actively engaging with companies, and supporting green bonds and impact investing, institutional investors can accelerate the transition to a low-carbon economy. Their commitment to sustainable investing, ESG reporting, and advocacy for supportive policies has the potential to drive positive change and make a significant contribution to addressing climate change and promoting responsible financial practices.

Green Technology Investments:

Driving Innovation for a Sustainable Future

Green technology investments refer to the allocation of capital towards projects, companies, and innovations that promote environmental sustainability and contribute to a greener, more sustainable future. These investments focus on developing and deploying technologies that address pressing environmental challenges, such as climate change, resource depletion, pollution, and biodiversity loss. Green technology investments play a crucial role in driving innovation, fostering economic growth, and achieving a more sustainable and resilient global society.

The Need for Green Technology Investments:

a. Climate Change Mitigation: Green technology investments aim to reduce greenhouse gas emissions and combat climate change. Innovations in renewable energy, energy efficiency, and carbon capture technologies are critical in achieving climate goals.

b. Resource Conservation: Green technologies help conserve natural resources by promoting efficient use and recycling. Sustainable agriculture, water management systems, and waste-to-energy processes are examples of resource-conserving innovations.

c. Biodiversity Conservation: Investments in green technologies that protect and restore ecosystems contribute to biodiversity conservation. Sustainable forestry, habitat restoration, and conservation technologies support efforts to protect the planet's rich biodiversity.

d. Resilience and Adaptation: Green technologies enhance society's resilience to environmental challenges by developing adaptive solutions to cope with climate impacts, such as extreme weather events and rising sea levels.

Key Areas of Green Technology Investments:

a. Renewable Energy: Investments in solar, wind, hydroelectric, geothermal, and biomass energy projects play a pivotal role in transitioning from fossil fuels to cleaner, renewable energy sources.

b. Energy Efficiency: Green technology investments focus on technologies and practices that reduce energy consumption in buildings, transportation, manufacturing, and other sectors.

c. Clean Transportation: Electric vehicles (EVs), sustainable aviation fuels, and public transportation systems are areas where green technology investments aim to reduce the environmental impact of transportation.

d. Circular Economy: Investments in technologies that promote a circular economy, where resources are reused, recycled, and repurposed, contribute to waste reduction and sustainable consumption.

e. Smart Grid and Energy Storage: Green technology investments in smart grid systems and energy storage technologies enable better integration of renewable energy sources and enhance grid reliability.

f. Sustainable Agriculture: Green technology investments support sustainable farming practices, precision agriculture, and agricultural technologies that reduce environmental impacts and increase productivity.

g. Green Building and Construction: Investments in green building materials, energy-efficient construction, and sustainable architecture drive more environmentally friendly urban development.

Role of Private Sector and Startups:

The private sector and startups play a crucial role in driving green technology investments. They often lead the way in developing and commercializing innovative green technologies. Through venture capital funding, private equity investments, and initial public offerings (IPOs), startups receive the necessary financial support to scale their green solutions and contribute to the transformation of industries.

Government Support and Policy Incentives:

Governments worldwide play a significant role in driving green technology investments. Policymakers provide financial incentives, grants, tax credits, and subsidies to support green projects and stimulate private investments. Government policies that set ambitious climate and sustainability targets create a conducive environment for green technology development and adoption.

Impact on Economic Growth and Job Creation:

Green technology investments have a positive impact on economic growth and job creation. As investments increase in renewable energy, clean transportation, and sustainable infrastructure, new job opportunities are created in the green technology sector. Moreover, green technologies spur innovation, productivity, and competitiveness, contributing to overall economic development.

Global Collaboration and Knowledge Sharing:

Green technology investments often require collaboration and knowledge sharing across borders. International partnerships, research collaborations, and technology transfers accelerate the global deployment of green technologies and help developing countries leapfrog to sustainable solutions.

Conclusion:

Green technology investments are vital for driving innovation and achieving a sustainable future. By supporting renewable energy, energy efficiency, clean transportation, circular economy practices, and other green technologies, investors, governments, and startups contribute to mitigating climate change, conserving natural resources, and fostering a more sustainable and resilient world. Embracing green technology investments not only addresses environmental challenges but also spurs economic growth, job creation, and technological advancement for the benefit of current and future generations.

Circular Economy and Sustainable Investments:

Closing the Loop on Resource Management

The circular economy is an economic model that aims to decouple economic growth from resource consumption and environmental degradation. It is based on the principles of designing out waste, keeping products and materials in use for as long as possible, and regenerating natural systems. Sustainable investments that support the circular economy focus on businesses, technologies, and projects that prioritize resource efficiency, waste reduction, and sustainable resource management. By promoting the circular economy, sustainable investments contribute to a more resilient, resource-efficient, and environmentally friendly economy.

Principles of the Circular Economy:

- **Design for Durability and Reusability:** Circular economy principles prioritize the design of products that are durable, repairable, and easily disassembled. This extends the product's lifespan and facilitates the reuse of components and materials.

- **Remanufacturing and Refurbishment:** In a circular economy, businesses engage in remanufacturing and refurbishment to extend the life of products and equipment, reducing the need for new resource extraction.

- **Recycling and Material Recovery:** The circular economy emphasizes recycling and material recovery processes to extract value from end-of-life products and convert waste into secondary resources.

- **Sharing and Collaborative Consumption:** Circular economy initiatives often promote sharing and collaborative consumption models, such as car-sharing or tool libraries, to maximize the use of existing resources.

The Role of Sustainable Investments in the Circular Economy:

- **Investing in Circular Business Models:** Sustainable investments support businesses that adopt circular economy principles, such as companies that focus on remanufacturing, product-as-a-service models, and circular supply chains.

- **Circular Infrastructure Investments:** Sustainable

investments target projects that develop circular infrastructure, such as recycling facilities, waste-to-energy plants, and systems for efficient material recovery.

- **Supporting Circular Innovations:** Sustainable investments provide capital for research and development of innovative technologies that enable circular practices, such as advanced recycling processes and eco-design tools.

- **Circular Startups and Entrepreneurship:** Sustainable investments are critical for supporting circular economy startups and entrepreneurs, helping them scale their businesses and drive market adoption of circular solutions.

Benefits of Circular Economy and Sustainable Investments:

- **Resource Efficiency:** Circular economy practices reduce the consumption of finite resources, leading to more efficient and sustainable resource management.

- **Waste Reduction:** By prioritizing reuse, remanufacturing, and recycling, the circular economy minimizes waste generation and the need for landfill disposal.

- **Climate Mitigation:** Circular economy practices contribute to climate change mitigation by reducing greenhouse gas emissions associated with resource extraction and manufacturing.

- **Economic Opportunities:** Sustainable investments in the circular economy create new economic opportunities, such as job creation in recycling industries and innovative business models.

- **Enhanced Resilience:** The circular economy enhances economic and environmental resilience by reducing dependency on scarce resources and mitigating the impacts of resource price volatility.

Circular Economy Policies and Regulations:

a. Extended Producer Responsibility (EPR): EPR policies make manufacturers responsible for the entire life cycle of their products, encouraging them to design products for easier recycling and material recovery.

b. Waste Management Regulations: Governments can implement policies that prioritize waste prevention, recycling, and sustainable waste management practices to support the circular economy.

c. Green Public Procurement (GPP): GPP policies require public sector entities to prioritize circular products and services in their procurement processes, driving demand for circular solutions.

d. Eco-Design Standards: Establishing eco-design standards encourages businesses to design products with circularity in mind, fostering a shift towards more sustainable and durable products.

Collaborative Efforts and Knowledge Sharing:

Collaborative efforts between governments, businesses, investors, and civil society are essential for advancing the circular economy. Knowledge sharing, best practice exchange, and international partnerships can accelerate the transition to a circular economic model globally.

Conclusion:

The circular economy offers a promising pathway to sustainable resource management, waste reduction, and environmental preservation. Sustainable investments that support circular business models, circular infrastructure, and circular innovations are key drivers in advancing the circular economy. By aligning investments with circular economy principles, investors contribute to a more resource-efficient and environmentally friendly economy. Implementing supportive policies and regulations further reinforces the circular economy's impact, enabling a more resilient and sustainable future for society and the planet.

Responsible Investment in Emerging Markets:

Challenges and Opportunities

Responsible investment in emerging markets refers to the practice of incorporating environmental, social, and governance (ESG) factors into investment decisions while considering the unique characteristics and challenges of economies in developing countries. It aims to promote sustainable development, address social and environmental issues, and encourage responsible business practices in these markets. While there are numerous opportunities for responsible investment in emerging markets, there are also specific challenges that investors must navigate to achieve positive outcomes.

Opportunities for Responsible Investment in Emerging Markets:

1. Sustainable Development: Emerging markets offer significant opportunities for investments that contribute to sustainable development. There is a growing demand for investments in renewable energy, clean technologies, sustainable agriculture, and infrastructure projects that support economic growth and environmental protection.

2. Social Impact: Investments in emerging markets can have a profound social impact by addressing issues such as poverty, education, healthcare, and gender equality. Responsible investors can support projects that improve the quality of life for local communities and promote social well-being.

3. Diversification: Investing in emerging markets provides diversification benefits for investors' portfolios. These markets often exhibit different growth dynamics and are less correlated with developed markets, offering potential risk reduction through portfolio diversification.

4. Access to Growing Markets: Emerging markets offer access to rapidly growing consumer bases and rising middle-class populations. Investing in companies with strong ESG practices can position investors to benefit from the growing demand for sustainable products and services.

Challenges of Responsible Investment in Emerging Markets:

1. Lack of ESG Data and Disclosure: One of the primary challenges in emerging markets is the limited availability of reliable and standardized ESG data. Companies may not disclose ESG information voluntarily, making it challenging for investors to assess their sustainability performance accurately.

2. Governance Risks: Emerging markets may face governance risks, including corruption, weak regulatory frameworks, and political instability. These factors can create uncertainty and affect investment decisions.

3. Environmental and Social Risks: Companies operating in emerging markets may face environmental and social risks, such as inadequate infrastructure, water scarcity, labor rights issues, and community relations challenges. These risks can impact the financial performance of investments.

4. Regulatory Environment: The regulatory environment in some emerging markets may not be conducive to responsible investment practices. Investors need to be aware of potential legal and policy barriers that could hinder sustainable investment initiatives.

ESG Integration and Risk Management:

To address the challenges and seize the opportunities of responsible investment in emerging markets, investors can focus on ESG integration and risk management strategies:

- **Thorough Due Diligence:** Conducting thorough due diligence is essential when investing in emerging markets. This includes analyzing the ESG performance of target companies and assessing potential risks related to governance, environmental practices, and social impacts.

- **Engagement and Active Ownership:** Engaging with companies and being actively involved in corporate decision-making can help drive positive change. Active ownership allows investors to influence companies to improve their ESG practices and address sustainability challenges.

- **Collaboration and Partnerships:** Collaborating with local stakeholders, governments, and other investors can help address ESG challenges effectively. Partnerships with local organizations and NGOs can enhance the impact of responsible investment initiatives.

- **Impact Measurement and Reporting:** Measuring the impact of responsible investments in emerging markets is crucial to demonstrate the value of sustainable practices. Robust impact reporting and transparent communication with stakeholders build trust and accountability.

Importance of Long-Term Perspective:

Responsible investment in emerging markets often requires a long-term perspective. Sustainable development and positive social impact may take time to materialize. Investors committed to responsible practices need to be patient and work towards building resilient and sustainable economies over the long run.

Conclusion:

Responsible investment in emerging markets presents significant opportunities to drive sustainable development, create social impact, and address environmental challenges. While there are challenges related to ESG data availability, governance, and regulatory environments, investors can overcome these obstacles through thorough due diligence, engagement, collaboration, and a long-term perspective. By incorporating ESG factors into investment decisions, investors can contribute to positive change and foster responsible business practices in emerging markets, promoting a more sustainable and inclusive global economy.

Green Real Estate:

Building a Greener and More Resilient Property Sector

Green real estate refers to the practice of developing, owning, and managing properties with a focus on sustainability, energy efficiency, and environmental responsibility. It aims to reduce the environmental impact of buildings and promote the well-being of occupants while enhancing the resilience of the property sector to climate change and resource challenges. Green real estate encompasses various sustainable building practices, green certifications, energy-efficient technologies, and eco-friendly designs that contribute to a more sustainable and resilient property market.

Sustainable Building Practices:

a. Energy Efficiency: Green real estate prioritizes energy-efficient designs and technologies, such as LED lighting, high-performance insulation, and energy-efficient heating, ventilation, and air conditioning (HVAC) systems. These measures help reduce energy consumption and lower greenhouse gas emissions.

b. Water Conservation: Sustainable buildings incorporate water-saving features, such as low-flow fixtures, rainwater harvesting systems, and water-efficient landscaping, to reduce water consumption and minimize the strain on local water resources.

c. Waste Reduction and Recycling: Green real estate encourages waste reduction during construction and promotes recycling initiatives within the property to minimize the environmental impact of waste generation.

d. Sustainable Materials: Sustainable building materials, such as recycled content, reclaimed wood, and low-impact products, are preferred in green real estate projects to reduce the use of non-renewable resources.

e. Indoor Air Quality: Green buildings prioritize indoor air quality by using low-VOC (volatile organic compounds) paints, formaldehyde-free materials, and efficient ventilation systems to ensure a healthier and more comfortable indoor environment for occupants.

Green Certifications:

a. Leadership in Energy and Environmental Design (LEED): LEED is a widely recognized green building certification program that evaluates buildings' environmental performance based on criteria such as energy efficiency, water conservation, indoor air quality, and sustainable site development.

b. BREEAM (Building Research Establishment Environmental Assessment Method): BREEAM is another popular green building certification that assesses the environmental performance of buildings and infrastructure projects worldwide.

c. Green Star: Green Star is an Australian green building certification program that evaluates the sustainability of buildings and communities.

d. EDGE (Excellence in Design for Greater Efficiencies): EDGE is an innovative certification system that helps developers assess and design green buildings with a focus on energy, water, and material efficiency.

Benefits of Green Real Estate:

a. Environmental Benefits: Green real estate reduces carbon emissions, conserves water resources, and promotes sustainable land use practices, contributing to climate change mitigation and environmental conservation.

b. Economic Benefits: Energy-efficient buildings result in lower operating costs due to reduced energy and water consumption. Additionally, green buildings often command higher rents and resale values, attracting environmentally conscious tenants and investors.

c. Health and Well-being: Green buildings provide healthier and more comfortable living and working environments, leading to improved occupant health, productivity, and well-being.

d. Resilience to Climate Change: Green real estate incorporates climate-resilient features that can withstand extreme weather events and changing climatic conditions, reducing risks to property owners and occupants.

Sustainable Neighborhoods and Communities:

Green real estate goes beyond individual buildings and extends to creating sustainable neighborhoods and communities. These developments focus on walkability, access to public transportation, green spaces, and mixed-use zoning to reduce car dependency, promote community interactions, and improve overall quality of life.

Policy Support and Green Incentives:

Government policies and incentives play a crucial role in promoting green real estate.

Tax incentives, grants, expedited permitting processes, and density bonuses are examples of policies that encourage developers and property owners to invest in sustainable building practices.

Investor Interest in Green Real Estate:

Sustainable and responsible investors increasingly prioritize green real estate as part of their investment strategies. By aligning with sustainable development goals and climate objectives, investors can contribute to positive environmental and social outcomes while achieving financial returns.

Conclusion:

Green real estate is a pivotal component of the broader sustainability agenda, promoting energy efficiency, environmental responsibility, and occupant well-being. By adopting sustainable building practices, pursuing green certifications, and creating resilient communities, the property sector can play a significant role in addressing climate change, conserving resources, and building a greener and more resilient future. Policymakers, developers, investors, and occupants all have a role to play in advancing the growth of green real estate and creating a more sustainable and resilient built environment.

Socially Responsible Bonds:

Financing Projects with a Social Mission.

Socially Responsible Bonds (SRBs) are a type of financial instrument that is issued to finance projects with a social mission. These bonds are part of the broader category of impact investing, where investors seek both financial returns and positive social or environmental outcomes. The primary objective of SRBs is to fund projects that address social issues and promote sustainable development, such as poverty alleviation, healthcare, education, affordable housing, clean energy, and more.

Here's a detailed explanation of Socially Responsible Bonds and how they work:

Purpose and Objectives:

SRBs are specifically designed to attract capital from investors who are committed to supporting social and environmental causes. The funds raised through these bonds are directed towards projects that aim to create a positive impact on society or address pressing social challenges. By investing in SRBs, investors can align their financial goals with their ethical and social values.

Issuer and Project Selection:

The issuer of SRBs can be governments, municipalities, supranational organizations, non-profit organizations, or corporations. These entities identify eligible projects that meet certain social criteria and have a clear positive impact on society. The projects may range from building sustainable infrastructure to financing social programs or initiatives that uplift marginalized communities.

Impact Assessment and Reporting:

Transparency and accountability are crucial in the SRB market. Issuers typically provide detailed information about the projects being financed, the expected social impact, and how the funds will be utilized. Additionally, there are independent organizations that may evaluate the social and environmental performance of these projects to ensure they meet the stated objectives.

Types of Socially Responsible Bonds:

- **Green Bonds:** These are a subset of SRBs that are specifically focused on funding environmentally friendly projects that address climate change and promote sustainability.

- **Social Bonds:** These SRBs finance projects that have a direct positive impact on social issues, such as education, healthcare, access to basic services, and poverty reduction.

- **Sustainability Bonds:** These bonds combine both green and social objectives, supporting projects that contribute to both environmental and social development.

Investor Attraction:

SRBs are designed to attract a diverse range of investors, including individuals, institutional investors, and impact-focused funds. With the growing awareness and interest in sustainable and responsible investing, SRBs have gained popularity in recent years.

Financial Returns:

Like traditional bonds, SRBs pay periodic interest to investors, and the principal amount is repaid upon maturity. The financial returns on SRBs are typically competitive with other bonds of similar credit quality, making them an attractive option for investors looking to combine financial gain with social impact.

Challenges:

While SRBs have the potential to drive positive change, there are some challenges that need to be addressed. These include defining and measuring the social impact, ensuring proper allocation of funds, avoiding "greenwashing" (where issuers exaggerate the social or environmental benefits), and maintaining transparency in reporting.

Regulation and Standards:

To ensure credibility and uniformity in the SRB market, there are various guidelines and standards that issuers may adhere to.

For instance, the International Capital Market Association (ICMA) has developed the Green Bond Principles and Social Bond Principles, which provide voluntary guidelines for transparency, disclosure, and reporting for SRBs.

In conclusion, Socially Responsible Bonds offer an innovative approach to mobilize capital towards projects that aim to address social challenges and promote sustainable development. By providing financial incentives for projects with a clear social mission, SRBs contribute to building a more socially inclusive and environmentally sustainable world.

Sustainable Agriculture Investments:

Promoting Food Security and Ethical Farming Practices.

Sustainable agriculture investments are a form of impact investing that aims to promote food security and ethical farming practices while considering environmental, social, and economic factors. These investments seek to support agricultural projects and practices that are environmentally friendly, socially responsible, and economically viable. The ultimate goal is to produce food in a way that preserves natural resources, protects ecosystems, and ensures the well-being of farmers and communities, both in the present and for future generations. Here's a detailed explanation of sustainable agriculture investments:

Environmental Sustainability:

Sustainable agriculture investments focus on practices that minimize the negative environmental impacts of farming. This includes reducing greenhouse gas emissions, conserving water resources, protecting biodiversity, and promoting soil health. Investments may support projects that employ techniques like agroforestry, crop rotation, cover cropping, precision farming, and organic farming, which help maintain the ecological balance and reduce the use of harmful chemicals.

Social Responsibility:

Ethical farming practices prioritize the well-being and rights of farmers, farmworkers, and local communities. Sustainable agriculture investments may target projects that provide fair wages, safe working conditions, access to education, and healthcare for agricultural workers. They also aim to support projects that involve local communities in decision-making processes and empower them to sustainably manage their resources.

Promoting Food Security:

Sustainable agriculture investments address the global challenge of food security by supporting projects that increase food production while ensuring the long-term availability of resources. These investments may focus on innovations that enhance agricultural productivity, improve post-harvest handling and storage, and develop drought-resistant or climate-resilient crop varieties. By promoting sustainable practices, investments contribute to the availability and accessibility of nutritious food.

Technological Innovations:

Sustainable agriculture investments often support research and development of innovative technologies that enhance farming efficiency and reduce environmental impacts. This includes investments in precision agriculture technologies, vertical farming, aquaponics, and other cutting-edge solutions that optimize resource use and reduce waste.

Value Chain Investments:

Sustainable agriculture investments may not be limited to on-farm practices. They can also include investments along the entire agricultural value chain, from production to distribution and consumption. This could involve supporting sustainable food processing, packaging, transportation, and retailing initiatives to ensure that the entire system adheres to ethical and environmentally friendly principles.

Impact Measurement and Reporting:

Like other impact investments, sustainable agriculture investments place emphasis on measuring and reporting their social and environmental impact. This involves setting specific sustainability targets and regularly assessing progress toward achieving them. Investors in sustainable agriculture projects often seek transparent and comprehensive impact reports to ensure that their investment is making a positive difference.

Regenerative Agriculture:

Regenerative agriculture is a key concept within sustainable agriculture investments. It goes beyond sustainability, aiming to revitalize ecosystems, rebuild soil health, and restore biodiversity. Regenerative practices, such as no-till farming, cover cropping, and rotational grazing, contribute to carbon sequestration and enhance ecosystem resilience.

Policy Advocacy:

Some sustainable agriculture investments may involve engaging in policy advocacy to promote supportive regulatory frameworks for sustainable farming practices. This can include lobbying for incentives, subsidies, or regulations that encourage the adoption of environmentally friendly and socially responsible farming techniques.

In summary, sustainable agriculture investments play a vital role in promoting food security and ethical farming practices. By supporting projects that prioritize environmental sustainability, social responsibility, and economic viability, these investments contribute to a more resilient and equitable food system that meets the needs of the present and future generations.

Climate Risk Analysis in Investments:

Assessing and Mitigating Environmental Risks.

Climate risk analysis in investments involves assessing and mitigating environmental risks associated with climate change. As the impacts of climate change become more evident, investors are recognizing that climate-related risks can have significant implications for financial performance and long-term sustainability. Climate risk analysis aims to identify and understand these risks to make informed investment decisions that consider both financial returns and environmental sustainability. Here's a detailed explanation of climate risk analysis in investments:

Understanding Climate Risks:

Climate risks refer to the potential adverse effects of climate change on investments. These risks can be categorized into two main types:

- **Physical Risks:** These are direct consequences of climate change, such as extreme weather events, rising sea levels, heatwaves, floods, and droughts. Physical risks can damage physical assets, disrupt supply chains, and affect the production and distribution of goods and services.

- **Transition Risks:** These arise from the transition to a low-carbon economy and the efforts to mitigate climate change. Transition risks include policy changes, technological advancements, shifts in consumer preferences, and market disruptions. For example, regulations promoting renewable energy may impact fossil fuel companies, causing stranded assets and financial losses.

Scenario Analysis:

Climate risk analysis often involves scenario analysis, which assesses how different climate-related scenarios may impact investments. Scenarios can range from a business-as-usual approach with high carbon emissions to a more sustainable pathway with significant emissions reductions. By considering various scenarios, investors can better understand the potential range of risks and opportunities associated with climate change.

Data and Models:

Climate risk analysis relies on climate data and models that project future climate conditions and potential impacts. These models help assess the likelihood and severity of climate-related events and provide insights into the regions and sectors most vulnerable to climate risks.

Integration into Investment Decisions:

Climate risk analysis aims to integrate environmental risks into the investment decision-making process. This may involve incorporating climate risk considerations into traditional financial analysis, risk assessment, and portfolio construction. Investors can use tools like Environmental, Social, and Governance (ESG) ratings and sustainability indices to identify companies with strong climate risk management practices.

Engagement and Disclosure:

Investors can engage with companies to encourage better climate risk management and disclosure. This involves dialogues with company management about their climate strategies, carbon emissions reduction plans, and resilience to physical climate risks. Furthermore, investors may advocate for improved climate-related disclosures in line with frameworks such as the Task Force on Climate-related Financial Disclosures (TCFD) recommendations.

Risk Mitigation Strategies:

Climate risk analysis informs the development of risk mitigation strategies. Investors may choose to divest from high-risk assets or companies that are not adequately prepared for the challenges of climate change. Instead, they may allocate capital to climate-resilient and sustainable investment opportunities, such as renewable energy projects or companies with strong adaptation measures.

Long-Term Perspective:

Climate risk analysis necessitates a long-term perspective on investments. Climate change is a gradual process with far-reaching consequences, and its impacts may unfold over decades. Investors need to consider how climate risks and opportunities may evolve over the long term when making investment decisions.

Collaboration and Collective Action:

Climate risk analysis often involves collaboration between investors, asset managers, policymakers, and other stakeholders. Collective action can amplify the influence of climate-conscious investors and drive positive change in industries and markets.

In conclusion, climate risk analysis in investments is a critical process for understanding and mitigating environmental risks associated with climate change. By integrating climate risk considerations into investment decisions, investors can navigate the challenges of climate change, seize opportunities in the transition to a low-carbon economy, and contribute to building a more sustainable and resilient financial system.

ESG Screening and Portfolio Construction:

Building Resilient and Responsible Investment Portfolios.

ESG (Environmental, Social, and Governance) screening and portfolio construction is an investment approach that incorporates environmental, social, and governance factors into the investment decision-making process. The goal is to build resilient and responsible investment portfolios that not only seek financial returns but also consider the broader impact on society and the environment. ESG screening and portfolio construction involve several steps to identify and include companies with strong ESG practices while avoiding those with poor ESG performance. Here's a detailed explanation of the process:

Understanding ESG Factors:

ESG factors refer to a set of criteria that assess a company's performance in three key areas:

- **Environmental:** This includes a company's impact on the environment, such as its carbon emissions, energy efficiency, waste management, water usage, and efforts to mitigate climate change.

- **Social:** This focuses on a company's impact on its stakeholders, employees, customers, and communities. Social factors may include labor practices, diversity and inclusion, community engagement, human rights, and product safety.

- **Governance:** This assesses the quality and effectiveness of a company's governance structures, such as board independence, executive compensation, transparency, and anti-corruption policies.

Screening for ESG Criteria:

ESG screening involves filtering companies based on their performance in the three ESG areas. Companies are typically categorized into three groups:

- **ESG Leaders:** These are companies that demonstrate strong ESG performance and exhibit responsible and sustainable practices.

- **ESG Improvers:** These are companies that show progress in improving their ESG performance over time.

- **ESG Laggards:** These are companies with weak or inadequate ESG practices.

The screening process can be conducted manually, but increasingly, there are ESG data providers and ratings agencies that assess and rank companies' ESG performance, making it easier for investors to identify suitable candidates for their portfolios.

Portfolio Construction:

After the ESG screening, the portfolio construction phase begins. Here, investors combine the ESG-screened companies with other traditional financial criteria to build a diversified and balanced investment portfolio. The goal is to achieve both financial returns and positive social and environmental impact.

Risk-Return Analysis:

Investors conduct a risk-return analysis to evaluate the potential financial performance of the ESG-focused portfolio. This analysis considers the ESG factors alongside traditional financial metrics, such as company fundamentals, valuation, growth prospects, and industry trends.

Engagement and Active Ownership:

Responsible investors often adopt an active ownership approach, engaging with companies in their portfolios to encourage better ESG practices. This involves dialogue with company management, filing shareholder resolutions, and participating in annual general meetings to influence corporate behavior positively.

Integration of ESG Across Asset Classes:

ESG screening and portfolio construction can be applied to various asset classes, including equities, fixed income, real estate, and alternative investments. As the awareness of ESG's importance grows, more financial products are being designed to meet different investor preferences and risk appetites.

Long-Term Perspective:

ESG-focused investing often takes a long-term perspective. Companies with strong ESG practices are believed to be better positioned to manage risks, adapt to changing market conditions, and deliver sustainable long-term performance.

Reporting and Transparency:

Transparent reporting is essential in ESG investing. Investors often seek clear and comprehensive disclosure of a company's ESG performance and progress toward sustainability goals. Similarly, investment managers provide reports on the ESG characteristics of their portfolios to clients.

Regulatory Landscape and Standards:

The regulatory landscape around ESG investing is evolving, with some countries introducing disclosure requirements and guidelines. Additionally, there are international standards and frameworks, such as the United Nations' Principles for Responsible Investment (PRI) and the Sustainability Accounting Standards Board (SASB), which provide guidance on ESG integration.

In conclusion, ESG screening and portfolio construction represent a growing trend in responsible investing. By integrating environmental, social, and governance factors into investment decisions, investors aim to build portfolios that align with their values, support sustainable practices, and contribute to positive social and environmental outcomes while seeking competitive financial returns.

Green Finance and Clean Energy:

Investing in Renewable Technologies.

Green finance and clean energy represent an essential aspect of sustainable investing, focusing on channeling capital towards renewable energy projects and environmentally friendly initiatives. Green finance involves the deployment of funds to support projects and companies that promote clean energy, reduce carbon emissions, and contribute to mitigating climate change. Clean energy refers to energy sources that have a lower environmental impact compared to traditional fossil fuels. Here's a detailed explanation of green finance and clean energy:

Green Finance and Sustainable Investing:

Green finance is a subset of sustainable investing, where environmental, social, and governance (ESG) factors are considered in investment decisions. In green finance, the focus is specifically on projects and initiatives that have a positive impact on the environment and contribute to a more sustainable future.

Investing in Clean Energy:

Clean energy refers to energy generated from renewable sources that have a lower environmental impact and are considered sustainable over the long term. Examples of clean energy sources include solar power, wind power, hydroelectric power, geothermal energy, and bioenergy. Investing in clean energy involves allocating capital to companies and projects involved in the production, distribution, and adoption of renewable technologies.

Renewable Energy Projects:

Green finance supports a wide range of renewable energy projects, such as:

- **Solar Energy:** Investing in solar projects involves supporting the installation of solar panels and solar farms that convert sunlight into electricity.

- **Wind Energy:** Funding wind energy projects contributes to the development of wind farms that harness wind power to generate electricity.

- **Hydropower:** Hydropower projects involve generating electricity by harnessing the energy of flowing or falling water.

- **Geothermal Energy:** Geothermal projects tap into the heat from the Earth's interior to produce electricity or provide heating and cooling.

- **Bioenergy:** This involves using organic materials, such as agricultural residues and organic waste, to produce renewable energy through processes like biomass and biogas.

Investment Vehicles for Clean Energy:

There are various investment vehicles available for investing in clean energy:

- **Green Bonds:** Green bonds are debt instruments issued by governments, corporations, or other entities to raise funds specifically for environmentally friendly projects, including clean energy initiatives.

- **Renewable Energy Funds:** These are mutual funds or exchange-traded funds (ETFs) that invest in companies engaged in clean energy production and related technologies.

- **Infrastructure Funds:** Some infrastructure funds focus on renewable energy infrastructure, such as wind farms and solar installations.

- **Venture Capital and Private Equity:** These investment vehicles may provide funding to early-stage clean energy startups and technologies.

Benefits of Clean Energy Investing:

Investing in clean energy offers several benefits:

- **Environmental Impact:** Clean energy projects help reduce greenhouse gas emissions and mitigate the impacts of climate change.

- **Energy Security:** Diversifying energy sources through renewables enhances energy security by reducing dependence on fossil fuels and imported energy.

- **Sustainable Growth:** Clean energy projects support sustainable economic development and job creation in the renewable energy sector.

- **Innovation and Technological Advancement:** Investment in clean energy encourages innovation and the development of new and more efficient technologies.

Challenges in Clean Energy Investing:

While clean energy investing is promising, it also faces challenges:

- **Regulatory Environment:** Policies and regulations can influence the growth of clean energy investments and impact project economics.

- **Intermittency:** Some renewable energy sources, like solar and wind, are intermittent, meaning they depend on weather conditions and may not provide a constant energy supply.

- **Initial Investment Costs:** The upfront costs of developing renewable energy projects can be significant, although they often have lower operational costs over time.

- **Market Competition:** The energy market can be competitive, and clean energy projects may face competition from established fossil fuel-based technologies.

In conclusion, green finance and clean energy investing play a crucial role in addressing climate change and transitioning to a more sustainable energy future. By allocating capital to renewable energy projects and environmentally friendly initiatives, investors contribute to reducing carbon emissions, promoting energy security, and supporting the growth of the clean energy sector.

The Role of Financial Institutions in Driving Sustainable Investments.

Financial institutions play a significant role in driving sustainable investments and advancing the principles of sustainable finance. These institutions, including banks, asset managers, insurance companies, and pension funds, have the power to influence capital allocation, promote responsible business practices, and contribute to achieving environmental and social goals. Here's a detailed explanation of the role of financial institutions in driving sustainable investments:

Capital Allocation and Investment Decisions:

Financial institutions control vast amounts of capital, making them crucial players in determining where investment funds are directed. By integrating environmental, social, and governance (ESG) factors into their investment decisions, financial institutions can direct capital towards projects and companies that demonstrate strong sustainability practices. This approach not only aligns with the institution's values and ethical considerations but also promotes long-term value creation and risk management.

ESG Integration and Reporting:

Financial institutions can actively integrate ESG criteria into their investment processes. This involves assessing the ESG performance of potential investments, engaging with companies on sustainability issues, and making informed decisions based on a combination of financial and ESG data. Additionally, financial institutions can provide transparent and comprehensive ESG reporting to their clients, demonstrating their commitment to responsible investing and promoting accountability.

Sustainable Product Offerings:

Financial institutions can design and offer sustainable investment products to meet the increasing demand from investors who seek to align their portfolios with their values. These products may include ESG-focused mutual funds, green bonds, sustainable index funds, and impact investing funds. By providing a range of sustainable investment options, financial institutions cater to diverse investor preferences and contribute to the growth of sustainable finance.

Engagement and Advocacy:

Financial institutions have the opportunity to engage with companies in their portfolios and advocate for sustainable business practices. Through active ownership, they can influence corporate behavior, support climate-related resolutions, and encourage companies to improve their ESG performance. Such engagement can lead to positive changes in corporate policies, risk management strategies, and sustainability disclosures.

Green and Socially Responsible Lending:

Financial institutions can shape sustainable investments through their lending practices. By providing loans and financing to projects that align with environmental and social goals, such as renewable energy projects, affordable housing, or sustainable infrastructure, they contribute to sustainable development and support the transition to a low-carbon economy.

Risk Management and Disclosure:

Incorporating ESG considerations into risk management practices enhances financial institutions' ability to identify and manage potential risks arising from environmental and social factors. This proactive approach allows them to better assess the long-term sustainability and resilience of their investments. Moreover, disclosing their exposure to ESG risks and their efforts to manage such risks provides transparency to stakeholders and investors.

Green Bonds and Sustainable Finance:

Financial institutions can be instrumental in promoting green finance by issuing and underwriting green bonds. Green bonds are specifically used to finance projects with positive environmental or climate benefits. By actively participating in the green bond market, financial institutions contribute to funding sustainable initiatives and mobilizing capital for climate-friendly projects.

Risk Awareness and Climate Stress Testing:

Financial institutions can conduct climate stress tests to assess the potential impact of climate change on their portfolios and operations. Understanding climate-related risks enables them to develop appropriate risk mitigation strategies and adapt to the evolving financial landscape shaped by climate change.

Collaboration and Industry Standards:

Financial institutions can collaborate with industry peers, policymakers, and NGOs to drive the development of sustainable finance standards, guidelines, and best practices. Participation in initiatives like the Principles for Responsible Investment (PRI) and the Task Force on Climate-related Financial Disclosures (TCFD) showcases their commitment to advancing sustainable investments and creating a more resilient financial system.

In conclusion, financial institutions have a pivotal role in driving sustainable investments and promoting responsible finance. Through capital allocation, ESG integration, sustainable product offerings, engagement, and risk management, they can influence positive environmental and social outcomes while contributing to long-term financial performance. Embracing sustainable finance principles not only aligns with global sustainability goals but also positions financial institutions as leaders in creating a more inclusive, resilient, and environmentally conscious financial system.

Impact Investing in the Corporate Sector:

Promoting Responsible Business Practices.

Impact investing in the corporate sector involves deploying capital in companies that demonstrate a commitment to responsible business practices and social and environmental impact. Impact investors seek both financial returns and positive social or environmental outcomes. By investing in companies that prioritize sustainability, ethical conduct, and stakeholder engagement, impact investors influence corporate behavior and contribute to driving positive change. Here's a detailed explanation of impact investing in the corporate sector:

Alignment with Impact Goals:

Impact investors have specific social and environmental goals they aim to achieve through their investments. These goals could include promoting clean energy, supporting gender equality, improving healthcare access, advancing education, reducing carbon emissions, or addressing other pressing global challenges. The investments are carefully selected to align with these impact objectives.

ESG Integration:

Environmental, Social, and Governance (ESG) factors play a crucial role in impact investing. Companies' ESG performance is evaluated to understand their approach to sustainability, social responsibility, and corporate governance. Impact investors assess how companies manage their environmental impact, treat their employees and communities, and maintain strong governance structures.

Active Ownership and Engagement:

Impact investors often take an active ownership approach by engaging with the companies they invest in. This involves active dialogue with corporate management to influence and encourage responsible business practices, transparency, and improved ESG performance. Through voting on shareholder resolutions and participating in annual general meetings, impact investors can advocate for positive change within the corporate sector.

Sustainable Business Models:

Impact investors prioritize companies with sustainable business models that create long-term value for all stakeholders, not just shareholders. Companies that consider the interests of employees, customers, suppliers, communities, and the environment are seen as more attractive investment options.

Social Impact Measurement and Reporting:

Impact investors place a strong emphasis on measuring and reporting the social and environmental impact of their investments. This involves setting clear impact metrics, tracking progress, and reporting the outcomes to stakeholders. Transparent reporting ensures accountability and allows investors to understand the real-world effects of their investments.

Stakeholder Engagement:

Impact investors consider the perspectives of various stakeholders, including employees, customers, local communities, and non-governmental organizations. Companies that prioritize stakeholder engagement and incorporate diverse perspectives are more likely to receive impact investment.

Supporting Impact-Focused Initiatives:

Impact investors seek companies that are involved in initiatives and projects with a clear social or environmental mission. These initiatives could involve community development, sustainable supply chain practices, philanthropic efforts, or partnerships with NGOs to address specific social or environmental challenges.

Measuring Financial and Impact Returns:

Impact investors evaluate both financial returns and impact performance. While financial returns are essential for the sustainability of impact investing, impact investors also assess how their investments contribute to positive change. Balancing financial and impact considerations ensures that investments align with the overall mission of generating positive societal and environmental benefits.

Fostering Innovation and Inclusivity:

Impact investors often support companies that promote innovation and inclusivity. These companies might be developing innovative products or services that address societal needs, and they prioritize diversity and inclusion within their workforce and leadership.

In conclusion, impact investing in the corporate sector goes beyond traditional financial considerations. Impact investors seek to promote responsible business practices by investing in companies that align with their social and environmental impact goals. By actively engaging with these companies, measuring impact performance, and supporting sustainable business models, impact investors drive positive change within the corporate sector and contribute to a more sustainable and inclusive economy.

Sustainable Development Goals (SDGs) and Finance:

Mobilizing Capital for Global Impact.

The Sustainable Development Goals (SDGs) are a set of 17 global goals established by the United Nations in 2015. These goals address various economic, social, and environmental challenges faced by the world, with the ultimate aim of achieving sustainable development by 2030. Sustainable development encompasses meeting the needs of the present generation without compromising the ability of future generations to meet their own needs. Finance plays a critical role in mobilizing capital and resources to achieve the SDGs. Here's a detailed explanation of SDGs and finance:

The 17 Sustainable Development Goals:

The SDGs cover a wide range of issues, including poverty eradication, hunger, health and well-being, quality education, gender equality, clean water and sanitation, affordable and clean energy, decent work and economic growth, industry innovation and infrastructure, reduced inequalities, sustainable cities and communities, responsible consumption and production, climate action, life below water, life on land, peace, justice, and strong institutions, and partnerships for the goals.

Mobilizing Capital for SDGs:

Achieving the SDGs requires significant financial resources. The estimated annual cost to implement the SDGs in developing countries alone is in the trillions of dollars. Mobilizing capital from various sources is essential to fund projects and initiatives that support the SDGs.

Public Finance and Official Development Assistance (ODA):

Public finance, including government budgets and official development assistance from donor countries, plays a vital role in financing SDGs. Governments can allocate funds to programs and projects that directly contribute to the achievement of the goals. ODA provides financial and technical support to developing countries for sustainable development projects.

Private Sector Investment:

Private sector investment is a major driver of financing for the SDGs. Impact investors, institutional investors, and corporations are increasingly recognizing the importance of aligning their investments with sustainable development objectives. They invest in companies and projects that contribute positively to the SDGs while seeking financial returns.

Blended Finance:

Blended finance involves combining public and private funds to finance SDG projects. It leverages the strengths of both sectors to address market failures and attract private investment to sectors with significant social and environmental impact.

Green Finance and SDGs:

Green finance focuses on directing capital towards environmentally sustainable projects that contribute to climate change mitigation and adaptation. Many of the SDGs, such as clean energy, sustainable cities, and climate action, are aligned with green finance principles.

Social Impact Investment:

Social impact investors allocate capital to projects that generate positive social outcomes, such as poverty alleviation, improved healthcare, and quality education, which are directly related to several SDGs.

Sustainable Banking and Finance Initiatives:

Financial institutions play a crucial role in mobilizing capital for the SDGs. Many banks and financial organizations have launched sustainable finance initiatives, including green bonds, social bonds, and sustainable development bonds, to fund projects with positive environmental and social impacts.

SDG-Linked Financing:

Some financial instruments are directly linked to the achievement of specific SDGs. For example, SDG-linked bonds have terms that tie financial returns to the attainment of certain SDG-related targets.

Impact Measurement and Reporting:

Transparent reporting and impact measurement are critical in SDG financing. Investors and financial institutions need to track the outcomes of their investments to ensure they are making a positive contribution to the SDGs.

Global Partnerships and Multilateral Development Banks (MDBs):

Global partnerships, such as the United Nations Development Programme (UNDP) and the World Bank Group, play a significant role in mobilizing finance for the SDGs. Multilateral development banks provide financial resources and technical expertise to support projects in developing countries.

In conclusion, the SDGs provide a comprehensive framework for addressing global challenges and promoting sustainable development. Finance is a key enabler in achieving these goals by mobilizing capital and resources from various sources. Public and private sector investments, green finance, social impact investment, and innovative financial instruments are essential tools in funding projects that contribute to the SDGs and creating a more sustainable and equitable world.

Green Innovation Funds:

Supporting Environmentally-Focused Startups and Ventures.

Green Innovation Funds are investment vehicles that focus on supporting environmentally-focused startups and ventures. These funds play a crucial role in financing and nurturing early-stage companies that are developing innovative solutions to address environmental challenges and promote sustainability. Green Innovation Funds seek to generate financial returns while also driving positive environmental impact. Here's a detailed explanation of Green Innovation Funds and their significance:

Investment Focus:

Green Innovation Funds specifically target companies and projects that are dedicated to finding solutions to environmental problems. These could include startups working on renewable energy technologies, sustainable agriculture, clean transportation, waste management, water conservation, and other eco-friendly initiatives.

Funding Early-Stage Companies:

Many environmentally-focused startups face challenges in accessing traditional financing due to the high-risk nature of their ventures. Green Innovation Funds fill this gap by providing early-stage capital to these companies, enabling them to develop and scale their innovations.

Supporting Innovation and Research:

Green Innovation Funds encourage research and development in the field of environmental sustainability. By investing in startups that are pursuing innovative solutions, these funds play a role in advancing technology and knowledge to address pressing environmental issues.

Impact Measurement and Reporting:

Green Innovation Funds typically have a strong focus on impact measurement and reporting. They assess not only the financial performance of the startups they invest in but also the environmental outcomes and contributions to sustainability goals. Transparent reporting ensures accountability and helps investors understand the real-world impact of their investments.

Venture Capital and Seed Funding:

Green Innovation Funds often operate as venture capital funds or seed funding providers. They offer equity investments or convertible debt to startups in exchange for a stake in the company, and they actively support the growth of these companies through mentorship, networking, and strategic guidance.

Partnerships and Collaboration:

Green Innovation Funds may collaborate with universities, research institutions, and government agencies to identify promising startups and leverage expertise in the environmental sector. These collaborations can enhance the funds' access to cutting-edge research and technology.

Portfolio Diversification:

Green Innovation Funds typically build diversified portfolios of environmentally-focused startups. This diversification spreads risk and increases the chances of supporting successful ventures that can have a substantial positive impact.

Alignment with Sustainable Development Goals (SDGs):

Many Green Innovation Funds align their investment strategy with the UN Sustainable Development Goals (SDGs), particularly those related to climate action, affordable and clean energy, responsible consumption, and sustainable cities and communities.

Positive ESG Screening:

Environmental, Social, and Governance (ESG) criteria play a crucial role in the selection of startups for investment. Green Innovation Funds seek companies with strong ESG practices and a clear commitment to sustainability.

Catalyzing Private Investment:

By supporting early-stage environmentally-focused startups, Green

Innovation Funds play a catalytic role in attracting follow-on investment from other private investors, venture capital firms, and impact-focused funds.

Long-Term Impact:

Green Innovation Funds recognize that addressing environmental challenges requires a long-term perspective. They support startups with the potential for scalable and lasting impact in their respective fields.

In conclusion, Green Innovation Funds are an essential part of the sustainable finance landscape, focusing on supporting startups and ventures that are at the forefront of addressing environmental challenges. By providing early-stage capital, mentorship, and support, these funds contribute to the development and growth of innovative solutions that promote environmental sustainability and drive positive change in the world.

www.ingramcontent.com/pod-product-compliance
Lightning Source LLC
Chambersburg PA
CBHW072205290526
45794CB00004B/1652